"We don't mind to lose a good applicant,
but definitely not hire a bad applicant."

I0011352

Get a Job without an Interview

-- Google and Beyond

Santosh Avvannavar
Raghavendra Kumar Reddy

Published by
Santosh Avvannavar
santosh.avvannavar@gmail.com

Powered by
Pothi.com
http://pothi.com

This book is dedicated to: -

The Almighty God,
Parents,
Pastor Anil and Sister Glory
(New Life Fellowship Church),
Dr. Meena R Chandawarkar,
Students
&
In Memory of Amrita R Chandawarkar

Acknowledgement

We would like to thank the Almighty God for giving us the ability to pen stories in his glory. We thank our parents for their unconditional love and support. We express our gratitude to our best friends Sameer Mirji, Vasudha Mirji, Amresha M, for being there during our times of trials. We also extend our gratitude to our mentors Meena R Chandawarkar, P V Ramana, N K Narasimhan; Suchita Khanna, Avinash Himanshu, Rahul Nair (motivators). We also thank Dr. Lokesh Patil (M.D.), Vineet Singh (Software Engineer at TCS), Saurav Kumar (MBA), Sachin K and Nithish J (Software Engineer at IBM) for their constant support.

We also extend our thanks to all the reviewers for the novel 'Adhuri Prem Kahaniya', and 'Dear Wife, Your Husband is not a Superhero', and 'Second Heart.' We also thank Amrita Foundation for HRD (www. amritafoundation.wordpress.com) for allowing us to pen our thoughts since May 2012. We thank Pothi. com team for their effort in making this book elegant and beautiful. Last but not the least to all our dear students!

Acknowledgement

Contents

Introduction

Software industry is relatively younger in comparison to various other engineering practices such as civil, chemical, manufacturing and others. Being newer, one can expect constant changes. An ability to adjust to this change by continuous learning with inclination toward logic, reasoning and soft skills will be a key point to remain afloat in this industry. For a student, college is the best place to get a best job or be an entrepreneur. One can look forward to creating communities related to Computer Engineering to learn and relearn. This book brings various such views of learning. The book takes the reader through various hiring practices (Section 1 and 3) in the best of companies to show the projection of constant change. For example, students' hands on experience from 'Open Source' would be looked as a default in the resume.

The book presents the various effects and side effects of an applicant's preparation for a job and career. Authors emphasize on 'Career preparation' over 'Job preparation', as getting a job is just a beginning of the honeymoon time. Through this book, we have attempted to provide an approach or framework, which will help in continuous learning. Part I presents layouts of hiring practices for some of the best software companies; this is provided to give an idea. However, roles and skills may change hence it's suggested readers refer to the company's career page to get the current details. Part II presents layouts on how one can get on the platform of continuous learning and practice to get that 'Dream Job' or start your own 'Gig'!

Part I

Overview on Traditional & Emerging Hiring Process

Our research and close observation of the job interviewing process for graduates at Indian Institute of Science, Bengaluru during 2008 and 2009 for nearly 500 students in various companies, is the inspiration for this book. The success or failure in job interviews to a certain extent is not in the candidate's hand. The challenge many applicants faced was that they didn't know what the interviewer was looking for apart from a 'Job Description' (JD) and 'Position Title'. The whole interviewing strategy is behind a closed door and perhaps it's not good news for applicants.

There are some known (controllable) parameters such as smile, firm handshake, business attire, or technical know-how in which the applicant may be well prepared. Though many companies claim they test the natural behavior of an applicant, most of the time applicants are forced to play the game expected by the hiring team. Some applicants are good at agreeing and nodding at all the assumptions of interviewers; that makes them be successful at interviews at times. The bottom line is that, if this is the way companies play a game, interviewees need to learn to respond that way. Hiring companies have many pre-assumptions of applicant's skills and competencies.

The first part of the book deals with different roles offered to freshers (less emphasis is given for lateral hiring) and their hiring process in companies such as Yahoo!, Google, Microsoft, Amazon, and Adobe. Although the information provided here is more specific for **IT product companies,** it is also a compilation of interview processes with shortlisted and successful applicants from various organizations.

This handbook is intended not to just help crack interviews but enable passionate computer seeking applicants or professionals (testers or developers in specific and other roles in general) to build their career. This handbook is unlikely to be obsolete for at least a decade, as large multinational companies will continue to adopt similar hiring process over small and medium companies. This is meant to say that there is a sandwiched trend in interviewing process for small companies through coding events, apprenticeship, trial weeks (66% hire rate success claimed by David Rusenko, Co-Founder, CEO, President, Weebly), projects contributors (contribution to open source) and assignments to check various skills and culture fitment. Some of these expectations are going to be default check marks that need to be highlighted in the resume to get an interview invitation. Although, as mentioned, large MNCs might not opt for the hiring methodologies preferred by medium and small hiring since it may be difficult to implement due to large-scale operations of these companies across continents but they may explore these options for lateral hiring in future.

If you are inclined towards programming, you should look forward to working for the top IT companies, because of their fascinating hiring process, work culture, opportunity to work with the best of talents and remarkable career growth. It is common for passionate programmers to put in 12-15 hour days to complete tasks. According to Erik Sanberg-Diment, there are three good reasons for a programmer to love programming by learning, observing and practising —first, to develop software that is unavailable or customize available software for suitable needs. Second, it's fun to program if one likes to lick-tickle puzzles and third, the mind exercise (such as logic skills and learning to learn) can be a pleasurable experience. We shall explore some of the roles offered, hiring processes, interviewee expectations, and expected outcomes in this book.

Section 2

Hiring and Arranged Marriage Analogy

We shall bring some philosophy, analogy and fiction to this section. We all have dreams, and not only the ones that are dreamt in sleep. The dreams to make it big! Chasing dreams! Let's take a couple of examples to understand the idea behind 'make it big' or 'chasing dreams'. The first example, Abraham Lincoln. If one asked who he is, a loud voice would come from any corner – 'ex- President of USA'. If one is asked, what was he before being the president? Perhaps a big silence. The answer to the latter: he was a 'clerk' at a patent office. If he hadn't dreamt to become 'The President', he would have retired with some higher department, grandpa to some children and based on his deeds he would be in heaven or hell. His story could have ended there. There is absolutely nothing wrong with it! He chose to do something else that could inspire generations to come.

Let us consider another example, Helen Keller. The moment one hears her name, you recollect a lady who was blind. Some of them may know that she was also deaf and dumb. What can one expect of such a person? Sympathy and empathy! Even, she chose to have non-fiction life through her renowned writing. These two are frequent examples, offered by motivational speakers to make people understand the depth of 'make it big' or 'chasing dreams.' They just didn't believe only in the outcome, but as well in the process. We assume that our readers are in this mode of chasing dreams; we now take you to a section on an interesting analogy on, 'How hiring process is similar to Indian traditional arranged marriages?'

Let's look into the general hiring process of most companies, who usually follow similar structures (with slight differences) to hire an applicant for a position.

Screening Resume: In Indian arranged marriages; the families send photographs of a girl to the boys' family and the boy's photo to the girls' family with a short summary. Similarly, companies too provide job designation, job description (JD), and some background of the organization. The applicant looks into the requirements and on finding a match sends the application via email or postal (with or without a referral). The well-structured resume with clear objective and technical emphasis is vital. Even if the requirement fitment is minimal, it is seen that candidates tend to apply; this is seen as well in arranged marriages as well. Let's see if the boy or girl would be good to see and/or to meet. This attitude is in our blood!

Aptitude Test: If both families feel satisfied, the boy's family is invited over. The boy (aspiring bridegroom) is welcomed and greater hospitality is desired from the family members. Companies on the 'JD' match would invite candidates for a single or combination of aptitude tests (General or Technical or combination).

The girl's (aspiring bride) family members are on the giving side and the boy's family on the receiving side. A merciful scene! All members of the boy's family wait to see the girl (aspiring bride) to walk in with the tea tray (mostly prepared the first time by the girl or maid in the kitchen). Lot of reactions can be observed; if there are smiles then a sigh is seen among the girl's family members. Similarly the test would define the next step into the hiring process.

Group Discussion: Often seen on such occasion, 'Mama's' (uncle's) are created on both sides of the families. Companies often put team members to hear the arguments or debates or talks or discussions of a general or specific format of 'Group Discussion'. The checklist is ticked against as the talk progresses in hiring and marriages as well. 'Mama' is a like a referee of a game to control the arguments. As the boy's family members are on receiving side, they are often seen to dominate. This situation is similar among many applicants who have a fear of rejection that makes one humble and modest, similar to the condition of the girl's family. Mostly people are rejected on the grounds of dominance, lack of articulation, not comprehending the expectations of the receiving side, and other unknown parameters.

Screening Interviews: Once the applicant makes it through the group discussion, the recruiter (interviewer) would like to ensure the applicant is passionate for the role applied. The applicant is invited for small talk. The same holds good in pre-arranged marriage discussions as well. Once everyone's ego is satisfied, both the family members realize it's a marriage (communion) of their boy and girl. Generally the boy's 'Mami' (aunt) would say, 'just have a look at the girl.' The boy seated at a distance, would try to pass off a stern look. The girl's 'Mami' (aunt) would slowly try to cajole the girl to look at the boy. The bride would lift her head; there are two possible extreme reactions (shy or oh God!). If the face didn't light up, it means 'No-No'. The acceptation or rejection is quite often clear from the face or expression of the interviewer.

Psychometric Assessments: If the reaction on the face is a 'yes', then family members will decide to leave the boy-girl to indulge in a private chat. The girl being (tender or expected to) shy, it's often the boy who initiates the talk. In general talks, the girl tries to ask serious questions, 'Did you have any girl friend(s)?' Based on the personality of the aspiring bridegroom (boy) and his honesty level, the girl may experience different emotions. There is a price tag to every honesty level! Companies often use tools (Psychometric assessments) to understand the personality fitment to the work culture and other factors. It's highly advised the applicant try and be natural in such assessments.

Technical Interviews: On learning that the girl and boy have similar interests, some people (mostly aunts, uncles, and neighbors) would like to test (education, ability to read) the girl through reading newspaper (often this ability is partially checked in the aptitude round), questions on cooking (core subjects) and future plans (career growth aspirations). These rounds are often tiresome for the applicant, and unexpected (well prepared or unprepared) subjects discussed and it surprises the preparation level against the desired level of the hiring team.

HR Interview: Although the process of two family unions has been promising, families often like to seek a final approval from other senior members of the family (Grandpa or Grandma or relatives living across the seas). They would also attempt to talk over the phone (telephonic interviews) or face-to-face (CEO or Business Head or HR) to confirm. For entry-level positions, there is less room for negotiation although one may check that in the process of hiring.

Job Offer: Once the families seek approval from the head of family (Business Head or Vice-President), a marriage date (joining date), invitation card (offer letter with specific information for the role hired) and supervision of minimal boy-girl meetings until the nuptial is tied (follow up till joined) is observed.

Reference Check and Background Verification: The families often do various reference checks like the work place of the bridegroom. To check the genuineness of education levels, character seen and heard (and records in the local police station), past employers (if approved by the applicant) and others.

On Role: There is often an excitement; expectations and dreams are set on the offer letter and the first day on the job, one needs to take into account that it's just a first night of the marriage.

Induction: Every organization is expected to provide induction to the hired employee's to orient them to the organizational goals. It's a phase of being in cloud nine! It's no less than a 'honeymoon' period.

Post-induction and thereafter: Challenges manifold as one progress in career (similar for the housewife as she is no more a bridegroom) – as there are ample comparisons, bias and hindrances in any projects. One needs to review performance and set goals (like the number of children, house to be purchased, car to own) to move to the next career level. To make it big, self-brand creation is vital in career progression. In the process of self-brand creation, identification of strengths and limitation is to be never overlooked. This would help to equip with new skills (being modest and compassionate to each other in marriages) to get into the next level in the career ladder.

Section 3

Make it Big!

This section discusses about various technical roles (not completely) offered by Yahoo!, Google, Microsoft, Amazon, and Adobe. Interview structures of these companies are provided although these aren't exhaustive; hence one needs to refer other resources mentioned in the reference section. The diagram below gives an overview of roles offered under software development, testing and systems.

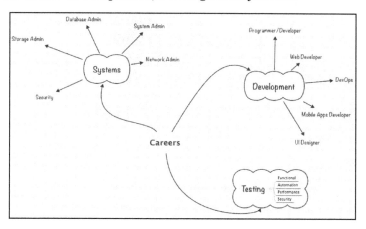

3.1 Roles and Interview Structure at Yahoo!

Yahoo! does characterization of roles for fresher or beginners under global job leveling criteria such as 'Individual Contributor.' An individual is expected to accomplish results by using expertise gained through university education to predominantly serve Yahoo! The general eligibility criteria are percentage cut off of 70% or CGPA 7; prefer B.E. (CS, IS, EEE, E&C, IT), MTech, MCA, MSc and MSc dual degrees. Yahoo! also provides opportunities for other streams of specialization, but candidate should have done courses in Data Structures, Programming Languages, Algorithms and Computer Architecture. Yahoo! India conducts subjective test, programming test, technical interview-1 and technical interview-2 (at times technical interview-3) and HR interview.

Each round is likely to be screening round at many a time. The recruiting team in general consists of Hiring Manager, Cross-functional partner, Functional or Technical expert, Next-level Manager and at times High-level leader to sell the role to the promising applicants. Yahoo! offers the following six broad areas for engineers –

Focus is IT roles:
1. Testing

2. Development

3. Release Engineer/ Dev Ops

4. dBA

5. System Admin

6. Storage Admin

   (dBA, System and Storage falls under Ops)

Yahoo! India does characterization of roles for fresher or beginners. Yahoo! India looks into detailed or minimum pre-requisite and they are checked in a narrow set during interview or test questions. Yahoo! offers the following roles for engineers-

Roles and Skills
Developer aka Dev. (or Field Engineer)
Skills (Basic or Mandatory): HTML, JS, CSS
If a developer likes to work as 'Web Developer', the following additional skill sets are needed-
Role: Web Developer
Skills: PHP or RAILS or Java Frame Works or Asp. Net or Django (Python)

If a developer likes to work as "Cloud Engineer", the following additional skill sets are needed-
Role: Cloud Engineer
Skills: Java (Core) or Python

Developer (In General)
Skills (Basic or Mandatory): Java or C/C++ or .Net
Additional Skills (Not Mandatory): API and Java (Core)
C/C++ is redundant and relying completely on them is not a good choice for developers.

Mobile Developer
Skills (Basic or Mandatory): HTML, JS, CSS
Additional Skills (Preferred): Java (Android) or .Net (Windows) or Objective C (ios)

Cloud Engineer
Basic (Basic or Mandatory): .Net, Java, Python, RAILS

A cloud engineer works on an interesting environment and is expected to learn and /or work on the following environments

1. OS - LINUX or Windows

2. Build - Ant or Maven

3. Unit Testing - Junit or Xunit

4. IDE - Eclipse or Visual Studio

5. dB - MySQL or PgSQL

6. Web Server - Apache or Tomcat

7. SCM - SVN or Git or Perforce

8. Scripting - Perl or Python

For the positions of Tech support, the skills sets are similar like Developer.

Testing
Test Engineer (Automation Engineer)
One might work on mobile, web, application or cloud
Java, Python, JS and other
Skills (Basic or Mandatory):

Test Engineer (Advanced)
Additional Skills (Mandatory): Tools-Selenium; Scripting-Pearl or Python or Ruby

Performance Engineer
Additional Skills: jmeter
Added advantage if the aspirant is well versed with Java (Core) and .Net

IT Operations
Application or Dev Ops
Skills (Basic or Mandatory): OS - LINUX or Windows

1. System Admin - Through certification

2. dBA Engineer

3. Storage Engineer

4. Network Engineer

5. Security Engineer

In order to move from role 'System Admin' to 'Security Engineer', prior experience of 'System Admin' is a pre-requisite.

Interview Structure

The interviewer (face to face or telephone) is expected to do a rigorous assessment of the applicant's capabilities by asking relevant, fact-based and accurate information by giving a realistic preview of the job opportunity at Yahoo! This is done to ensure that an applicant should walk away as a Yahoo! promoter irrespective of the outcome of the interview. Perhaps this is followed at most of the top IT hiring organization or others might follow a similar suite.

Step1: Preparation   (10-15 minutes)

Interviewer spends 10-15 minutes by reviewing the job description, applicant's resume, and questions' preparation.

Step 2: Introduction   (5-10 minutes)

Interviewer is expected to introduce him/herself with a gesture (smile) and ensure that the applicant is comfortable. Talks about the role, history of Yahoo!

and interview tries to sell the opportunity. The possible topic an interviewer uses to sell is the Yahoo! position in the market (product launch, Yahoo! and competitors) or Best Place to Work (Industry awards, recognition) or Facts (Perks). Applicants are free to know more about the role. This step usually takes 5-10 minutes.

Before moving to step 3, there is first transition phase - during this phase interviewer explains about the interview format. Something like this, 'I will test with questions that are related to your experience and skills, and I would be having end goal (specific answers and examples).' This is done to check for role-fitment and you may feel free to ask questions. Do you need any further clarification? This transition phases and helps the applicant to understand the expectation.

Step 3: Questions Round

Interviewers are generally assigned with some focus area and they are expected to probe technical information provided by the applicant's with best examples to check those information provided in the resume. The skills assessed are technical skills, problem-solving approach, and creativity, thinking ability along with other soft skills such as team-player skills, motivation, values and others. During this step, interviewer focuses on the applicant's challenges in the area of technical experts or understanding. One can expect questions on Algorithms, Data Structures (RDBMS), and Networks and hands-on experience to write a code could be given to the applicants. This step takes about 30-45 minutes.

Before moving on to step 4, there is a second transition phase in which the interviewer allows for some time for applicant's to ask questions.

Step 4: Q's and Yahoo!

Irrespective of the previous step's outcome, applicants are given the opportunity to raise questions. Applicants should use this opportunity to re-work in case step 3 didn't seem promising. Interviewer would continue to sell the opportunity by giving a realistic job preview. This step consumes about 10 minutes.

Step 5: Closure & Summary

This step is mixed with a transition phase in which the interviewer thanks the applicant for their valuable time and interest in Yahoo!. The applicant is introduced to the next interviewer and informed about the next step in the hiring process. This step takes about 5 minutes.

Step 6: Evaluation and Document

The interviewer spends about 10 minutes to complete the interview feedback form. The interviewer suggests areas for the next hiring team member to probe further.

All these steps take between 60-95 minutes and this is likely to be repeated for the next round of hiring or interviews.

3.2 Roles and Interview Structure at Google

Google doesn't do characterization of roles for fresher or beginners. Google doesn't look into detailed or minimum pre-requisites like Yahoo!; rather they are checked in a broad set of interview or test questions. Perhaps Google believes in the philosophy if an applicant possesses an ability to work on the basics, they can learn the software languages or other project requirements on need basis in some stipulated time. Google offers the following five roles for engineers -

Software Engineer
Skills (Basic or Mandatory): Algorithms, Data Structure, Problem Solving
Note: There is no specific section on problem solving, however the approach and process is checked while interviewing the applicants.

Software Engineer Test
Skills (Basic or Mandatory): Algorithms, Data Structure, Problem Solving, Aptitude tests (Case Tests)

Application Developer
Skills (Basic or Mandatory): Java, C, C++, Data Structure

Site Reliability Engineer

Skills (Basic or Mandatory): Perl, Shell Scripting, Data Structure & Algorithms (Basics), Networking

User Experience Designer

Skills (Basic or Mandatory): Strong visual design skills, design ability, Design across multiple device types and context (mobile, accessories, desktop), Outstanding written and verbal communication skills.

Product Quality Analyst

Skills (Basic or Mandatory): Knowledge and understanding of Commerce risk, AdWords risk, Adspam, Search quality evaluation, Landing page site guidelines and Local search are vital for this role.

Google India is likely to conduct a written (subjective) test to assess the candidate before taking them through different technical rounds. Yahoo! India test may also consist of some objective and subjective questions. This format is generally seen in on-campus hiring. The advantage of on-campus would be to close the interviews on day 1 or 2, and to maintain cordial relationships companies tend to hire at least one candidate without diluting the hiring process.

The advantage of off-campus is that a written test is unlikely. This may have advantages for people not well proficient in written or timed tests among peer groups. The candidate for off-campus goes through one or two telephonic interviews before being invited for further interviews at the office premises. An applicant is likely to undergo three to five rounds on or off-campus interviews.

Some interesting scenarios during Google hiring –

1. If the panel 1, 2 and 3 selects a candidate then it is likely that s/he will not go for further rounds. High chances of being selected if a candidate are not invited for round 4 and 5.

2. If a candidate goes to round 4 and 5, then it is likely that s/he is on border decision (dilemma) but it doesn't mean the candidate cannot get through the interview process.

3. If a candidate is not found to be suitable after any round (say round 1), the interviewer feels or gets a strong notion of deviation from the applicant, the interviewer completes the assigned round. The information is passed on to Human Resource Manager and Senior Engineer about the interviewer views. They would further notify the

34

placement co-ordinator or placement cell for non-continuation of the next round to the candidates. This is handled with strong caution. Scenarios a, b and c are seen commonly during on-campus interviews.

4. During on-campus interviews, the interviewers generally tend to avoid giving feedback on each applicant interview to the interviewee's. Declines such requests politely; company policy doesn't allow us to share the feedback on the rounds. This perspective is right because it's hiring time, and not practice time to finetune after rounds. It's like a game; you win or lose at each round. Each player perhaps gets to know the outcome during the process.

5. Whereas during off-campus interviews, after the first telephonic rounds the applicants are checked for their ability of coding (provided online on Google docs) during the interview for Software Engineer position; whereas shell scripting or perl scripting is checked during Site Reliability Engineer Position (at office premises) where they would go through all the rounds assigned for the day. The company has to invest money and allocated resources for the day. A recruiter helps on arrival for a formal preparation for the day.

Applicants can discuss and get the information needed, as this is not an acceptance or rejection round.

6. The interviewers submit a detailed feedback (subjective) to the hiring committee for further information required to arrive at a decision. Each interviewer feedback is kept anonymous. The hiring committee forwards all the reviews to the Vice-President to make a final decision. During the decision making, the committee also looks into each interviewer profile or past history to understand the possible understanding of hiring decision done during those individual rounds for each interviewers.

3.3 Roles and Interview Structure at Microsoft

Microsoft hiring is based on four guiding principles and they are -

1. Hire the best is a top priority.
2. Hire based on qualifications and long term potential.
3. Every hire is for Microsoft first.
4. Committed to diversity in the workplace.

Microsoft offers the following roles in engineering division -

Design Research

Content Publishing

Game Design

Project Engineering

Product Planning

Software Development

Software Developer Engineering in Test

Service Engineering & others

At Microsoft the hiring manager forms an interview loop of 4 to 6 people to conduct the interviews for a specific role. One of the important goals for the entire interviewer team is to create a positive candidate experience of the team and for Microsoft. Generally the hiring team consists of a 'Recruiter', 'Hiring Manager', 'Interviewer', and 'Senior Team Member'. Each interviewer will be assigned to assess 2-5 competencies on average and in overall 10-15 competencies (out of 30+ competencies) are checked. A hiring manager can assign more than one interviewer to assess a specific competency of an applicant. An internal candidate undergoes 3 or 4 interviews, while an external candidate undergoes 4 or 6 interviews.

How does the interview day look like?

Recruiter meets the candidates, prepares the candidate for the interviews and conducts a competency-focused interview. The interviewers are active listeners; engage the applicant in conversation instead of inquisition. Interviewer takes notes discreetly and provides ample time to answer further questions an applicant might have. The interviewer thanks the candidate and ensures to inform the applicant about the next steps. As part of interview strategy, the interviewer is expected to finish on time and provides feedback by email and verbal on follow up. Microsoft believes in strong overall hire for the company and doesn't welcome just any fillers for the vacancy.

Interview Structure

Step1: Warm-Up/ Introduction and Opening (5 minutes)

An interviewer initiates the conversation by covering a broad topic of the candidate background.

For example -

Candidate resume

A typical day at office

Checking the primary responsibility for the hiring role

Why you find Microsoft appealing?

Your role in the latest project.

Step 2: Technical or Functional Knowledge and Skills Assessment (Time Vary)

The interviewer checks the applicants' demonstration on technical depth, problem solving, adaptability, and curiosity. Technical knowledge is assessed in areas like C++, COM, Internet, SQL, Multithreading, Visual Basic, Java and others. The level of questioning goes from Simple level 1 to Difficult level 3 for each question asked by using probing technique.

For example -

Level 1: What is the base interface?

Level 2: What are the members of an interface?

Level 3: What are some threading models?

Examples of Technical Interview Questions

When you look at webpage, is it faster to have one large image or many small images? Why?

What is the difference between locking and deadlocking?

What is the purpose of a class implementing an interface?

When is member initialization required?

What is the difference between class and a struct?

Is it possible to inherit and have member functions in a struct?

In multithreading, what is critical section?

Step 3: Competency Assessment (20-45 minutes)

The interviewer uses one behavioral and one hypothetical question and probing questions for 10-

15 minutes for each competency. Each interviewer is assigned to check 2-4 competencies of the applicants. Competencies checked fall broadly in the following categories -

Coaction: Working with team with ability to drive alignment across the organization.

Customer Focus: Ability to resolve the expectation by being proactive facilitates the required needs.

Drive for results: Effective use of problem solving skills to achieve the desired positive outcome.

Influencer: Ability to persuade, and influence others by effective communication.

Sagacious: Ability to develop far sightedness to scope the problems effectively via training or knowledge or learning with others to make effective positive decision.

Planning, Organizing and Executing: Ability to take initiatives to create and drive plans to implement various projects aligned to businesses need.

Technical or Functional Knowledge: Applies various principles to solve complex problems, ability to learn and use new methodology to incorporate in the work.

Flexibility: Ability to efficiently respond to the changing demands of the work. Ability to handle ambiguous situations, possess curiosity and constructive mindset.

Behavioral questions are used to describe the applicant's past behavior such as specific actions taken, contribution made and obstacles overcome. In case the applicant has less experience, hypothetical questions are used to check the applicant's responses to scenarios. The probing questions are used to drill down into behavioral questions for more detail, which allows more comprehensive assessment of the applicant. The probing questions help the interviewer to understand the applicant's breadth and depth. The interviews are generally open, interactive and mutually beneficial discussion with the applicant.

Examples of Behavioral, Hypothetical and Probing Interview Questions

1. How did you handle stress that was created because of major organizational change?

2. Tell me about a time when you experienced conflict with a team member.

3. Tell me about a time when you fell short of a customer's needs.

4. Tell me about the most difficult assignment or task in your career so far?

5. Give an example of a relationship that you developed through networking that had a positive impact on your work.

6. How did you handle the situation on learning you made a critical error in your work?

7. Tell me about a time you did not meet a planned milestone (goal) at work.

8. When and how did you improve in code, designs or content property?

Step 4: Question and Answers - Selling and Closing (10-15 minutes)

The interview is expected to maximize the perception of Microsoft as the employer of choice for the technical or business world.

Post step 4, the interviewer prepares a transcript of the applicants for their 'strength' and 'weakness'. Each interviewer in the interview loop provides feedback on the applicants by organizing feedback by competencies and technical or functional knowledge and skills. Each interview provides 'Hire' or 'No Hire' feedback in the feedback job aid sheet. The hiring manager takes the final decision based on the comprehensive assessment.

It is expected that applicants interviewed for a given position be asked the same set of targeted questions. As part of interviewing strategy, an interviewer is informed not to make any first impression, try to understand communication styles and preferences, never jump to conclusions and understand the cultural differences.

For example -

Soft Handshake

No eye contact

Spoken Accent

Excellent College or School

Won't initiate questions

What does Microsoft interviewer look in an applicant?

An interviewer checks an interviewee approach and solution to the problem, its not just about getting the right solution. There are wide number of challenges that can hinder an interviewee from identifying the optimal solution, this will help to understand the ability of interviewee possession for certain job-related competencies. Is it advisable for an interviewee to try multiple strategies, failure of some strategies? The failure isn't bad, but an interviewee should step back far enough to get back on track. This also helps the interviewer to check the ability of analysis, process and outcome of an interviewee.

3.4 Roles and Interview Structure at Amazon India

Amazon has vast operations, it offers various roles based on business needs of various teams. The following are the key positions that Amazon India offers for fresher or beginners under global job leveling criteria such as 'Individual Contributor.' An individual is expected to accomplish results by using expertise gained through university education to predominantly serve Amazon. The general eligibility criteria are percentage cut off of 70% or CGPA 7; prefer Bachelor's degree and/ or Master's degree (CS or relevant equivalent). Amazon India hires the best of talent from top institutions for Software Development and Quality Assurance apart from Support Engineer role. There are minimal opportunities for fresh graduate engineer for off- campus or lateral hiring, as one needs a minimum experience to get into level one role.

Amazon India conducts a test that includes two sections. The first section of the test is multiple-choice questions (about 20) and the second section comprises coding questions (about 2). In general, each test is an elimination round. There is a cut-off for the section one and applicant's need to be cautious as there is negative marking for each wrong answer! The first section consists of questions on coding, fundamentals of computer science, data structure, aptitude, and puzzles. The evaluation of coding is generally bucketed into categories that would define candidates ability to reach an expected bar. For example, the code is readable or no bug with the optimal solution shown etc. Followed this there will be three to five rounds or interview consisting of technical, managerial and HR rounds.

Amazon offers the following three broad areas for engineers-

Focus is IT roles:

1. Software Development

2. Quality Assurance

3. Support Engineer

Amazon offers the following roles for engineers -

Roles and Skills

a. Software Development Engineer Level I

Skills (Basic or Mandatory): Java or C++ in a Linux environment and familiarity with Perl or SQL

Preferred: Database modeling skills or experience with modeling data for cloud storage

Experience with mobile development

Distributed systems experience

Knowledgeable about security best practices

b. *Quality Assurance Engineer Level I*

This is one of the meaty and challenging roles for fresh graduate engineers. The aspirants need to have fair knowledge of software applications, software development, and quality assurance practices to check the code developed by Amazon to the highest quality by meeting all the requirements and provide a superior customer experience. One is expected to have a breadth of software lifecycle knowledge and software quality best practices.

Skills (Basic or Mandatory): Strong knowledge of QA methodology and tools, modern (latest) programming languages, ability to understand technical specifications and analyze log files with fair communication skills (verbal and written).

Preferred: Experience in Java or Perl or Python based automation and/or user-level

Experience in Unit Testing frameworks like Junit, HttpUnit

Knowledge of UNIX environment and Shell scripting

c. *Support Engineer Level I*

A support engineer is expected to troubleshoot, debug, evaluate and resolve computer-identified alarms, host management and automate routine operational tasks, perform software deployments and migrations. The team operates '24 x 7 x 365' manner and is likely to involve working in night shifts and on weekends in rotations.

Skills (Basic or Mandatory): UNIX base operating system experience, Scripting (Shell or Ruby or Perl etc), Debugging or troubleshooting, C or C++ or Java (familiarity), SQL queries (understanding), Verbal and written communication skills, Problem-solving, Decision-making ability, Proactive, Attention to details and ability to work in 24x7 on-call support.

Preferred: Knowledge of distributed applications or enterprise application.

Knowledge of Cloud technology.

3.5 Roles and Interview Structure at Adobe India

Adobe looks for highly talented and engaged people. Those with innovative bend of mind and achievements are at the right place to start off their career. Adobe takes candidate's interview experience seriously to measure how Adobe is perceived in the market. It goes to say that if 10 applicants are interviewed, 2 are likely to get the job and 8 will not. Experience of 8 candidates is crucial as this defines brand and reputation in the market. Each interviewer plays a vital role in positioning the organization.

Hiring Manager prepares for requisition to open a position in lieu with the Business partner. Then the recruiter will search for candidates that are best suited for the position. To provide opportunity to their internal employee's, the position is open internally for a while and external hirings are opened later. Hiring Manager prepares the questions with the recruiter with respect to the job responsibilities. The resumes are reviewed and a predictive model is prepared to check the expected outcome. The hiring manager will identify the interview panel and communicate to each interviewer with the focus area to interview. Once the rigorous assessment of the applicant is over, the feedback is collected from the interview panel to know the outcome.

Structure of the Interview

Adobe interviewer does briefing, explains the role for which you would be hired. (5-7 minutes)

Interviewer asks questions prepared prior to the day of interview. (25-30 minutes)

Candidates are given an opportunity to ask questions. (5 minutes)

The interview is concluded and the candidate is escorted to the next interview.

The interviewer spends some time documenting the feedback of the candidate assessed.

Adobe hiring team will check the applicants' various expertise such as –

1. Did the applicant have a similar function in the past or current role?

2. Does the applicant have relevant industry experience?

3. Does the applicant have strong functional expertise for the role to be hired?

4. Does the applicant have relevant technical skills such as SAAS environment testing, automation tools and others?

5. Does the applicant have promising background on accomplishment or achievements for the role to be hired?

6. Does the candidate have a minimum education?

7. Will the candidate be able to handle pressure or conflicts?

8. Does the candidate show ownership and accountability?

9. Does the candidate work on deadlines?

10. Is the candidate good at engaging by articulating his/her ideas?

11. Does the candidate showcase the logical ability towards problem solving?

12. Does the candidate fit in with Adobe work culture?

It is common to hear phrases like problem solving, testing, and robust code throughout the career hiring process. Let's examine what these terms really mean for many hiring companies:

What companies look for in candidates' responses – The candidate's approach and solution for any given problem. Remember, it's not about just getting the right solution. Various stumbling blocks or bottlenecks that an applicant is likely to encounter to arrive at the best solution are checked during those few minutes of the interview. The way the applicant approaches a problem may provide a basis to the interviewer for assessing whether the candidate demonstrates possession of certain job-related competencies.

The following keywords are checked –

Multiple Strategies

Identification of strategy

Route backing

Analysis (process and results)

Questioning/Clarification

Intelligent usage of hints

Section 4

Best Hiring

The applicants' transcript prepared by the interviewer that consists of 'strength' and 'weakness', are shown for a sample pool of candidates here:

Sample Transcript for Software Engineer Role

Applicant: Rahul

Strength:

a. Demonstrated ability to troubleshoot and solve the problem

b. Demonstrated functional understanding and skills

c. Showcased experience in running well defined test cases and ability to deal with issues

Weakness:

a. Promising for an individual contributor position, may not work in a team based on previous work related examples.

b. Did not communicate (clear and concisely) the thoughts in a clear pattern.

c. Did not showcase any examples of implementation of work for larger teams that is necessary for the environment.

Applicant: Anjali

Strength:

a. Demonstrated ability to work in a large team through passion towards the products of the previous organization.

b. Self-motivated to find ways to implement the tasks.

c. Demonstrated ability to work in a dynamic situation of the work environment.

Weakness:

a. Minimal functional knowledge because of limited scope in the previous role.

b. Needs functional support to see effective output for the needed work environment.

c. Would need to invest in training for 3 months or more in order to align to the business need.

Each interviewer provides their feedback with a final statement of 'Hire', 'No Hire', and 'No Hire –Fitment for other roles' to the Hiring Manager to take the final decision.

Part II

Section 5

Misconception to Programming

It has been observed (through workshops and training) that many students feel good or bad or not so good at programming even though they may have had good programming skills in college. Unfortunately, the education imparted at colleges doesn't bring the differences between the programming in an academic setup to programming at the work setup. This statement is true as programming itself is not a job of software professionals. Job descriptions are also biased in this aspect. Programmers do more than just write code. They need to gather requirements and analyze those requirements if not provided, work on endless design patterns to analyze the architecture, create test plans, evaluate and improve the quality of a system, work in intercultural groups with their different experience levels, provide rough to right estimation of work plan, and continuous communication with different needs of stakeholders through negotiation, quality, budget, and features to reach a possible agreement.

The educational set provides an isolated and well-defined problem with short decay time for the obtained result. Learners are exposed to tools prior to assignment and outcome is generally measured through desired output. This scenario barely (not yet all!) exists in the real world as the problem is complex, embedded deep in conceptual or context, requirements often change with time, and an agile solution is preferred to react to those changes. Learners learn tools themselves through available ones or create new ones. Regression and usability test runs would run, as improvement for software projects would never dry out. Hence the misconception which makes Computer Science (CS) students think that programming is all about software engineering, whereas the reality is that CS prepares students for real world software development like horse riding training would prepare an army for battle!

Section 6

Ways to Learn Programming

There is no one unique method to learn programming, but there are many best ways to deal with it. The one word that is frequently heard whenever it is asked about the best way to learn and be a good programmer is: 'Practice.' That's absolutely right! Practice encompasses remembrance. Let's deal first about this challenge; we often assimilate information as abstract. For example, my name is Ms. Rosy and it's true that often we would forget the name before the conversation ends. The conversion of abstract to visual information is one of the best ways to deal with remembrance. Let's take the same example, 'Rose' and 'Rosary'. The remembrance is often achieved by repetition (coding in different languages) of tasks. One will need to identify their ways of learning – a well-developed system or customize a system.

To master each sub-system, one will need to evolve step by step. For example, while playing football the coach teaches defense, offense and other mechanisms each at a time. There is no short cut, but there are better ways to learn programming. Computer

Engineers have to get this into their head all the time, 'Lawyers or doctors are known as practicing lawyers and doctors and engineers are no exception to this view.' Some of us might still have a question, how do we practice in the real world? According to Dave's, (www.codekatak.com) there are two things he puts in his blog. The first is the pressure free time (temporal oasis) with no deadline. He suggests that a relaxed attitude can help to learn by practice. The second is to seek flexibility to make mistakes, improvise, reflect and measure. Although there are thousands of programming languages, the following order can be helpful for beginners. The list of programming languages with no experience—

1. Java – It is a higher language, is compatible with any operating system.

2. Python – It is based on human readability in mind. (Heard of Django, NumPy ?)

3. Ruby – It is similar like Python but is less readable. (RAILS anyone!!)

4. C – Most widely used programming languages, very apt for beginners.

5. C++ - It acts like a bridge between C and Java.

6. HTML and CSS – These are essential for webpage design.

7. MIT App Inventor for Android – It requires no coding, shows programmers think tank and concepts in computing.

There are various next levels of languages that one can look to master as follow-up languages. We recommend the learners to stick to one language till they become comfortable with it.

1. C#

2. Objective-C

3. Java script

4. PHP

Let us consider case by case to understand possible ways to learn programming (not specific to particular programming languages) that allows one to do mistakes, improvise, and reflect and measure –

Step1: LearnPython (www.learnpython.org) (www.learn-js.org) (www.rubymonk.com)

One of the simplest formats of learning programming (with minimal pre-requisite of the Internet) with basic and advance tutorials made available online.

This gives a taste of language to ease the process of programming, quick to work or fix and re-work. Similar formats are available for other programming languages.

Step 2: Koans Method

A Koan comes from Zen Buddhism that consists of a dialogue, question, story or statement that can be accessible through intuition over rational thinking. Koans (such as Ruby Koans, Java Koans and others) have helped and made programming much easier to learn. There are a series of files; each file needs to fixed before moving to the next file. The file would look like as shown below-

(https://github.com/gregmalcolm/python_koans)

For example in Python:

1. def triangle (a, b, c);
2. # DELETE
    'PASS' AND WRITE THIS CODE
3. Pass

All the underscores (not shown above) need to be figured out and filled in. As the underscore gets the appropriate answers, the rake in one's terminal will help to check the answers otherwise. Koan uses notion of red, green and refractor (also known as test driven development) with each color being an indicator — red (fail), green (make the test pass), refactor (any other ways to improvise it?). There is relatively less programming involved (coding and articulation) and rake in the terminal would give away answer or clue, which is a possible disadvantage of this method, but it's a handy tool to pick up and learn the concepts.

Step 3: Exercism (www.exercism.io)

This uses the approach of Test Driven Development. In this, if a test fails, one will get an experience to test failures (by themselves and others) and fix those failures (by themselves and others). One can also rely on other feedback to gauge the importance of teamwork in this system. This step will provide an experience close to work experience and real time experience of working for someone.

Step4: GitHub
(www.github.com/thekarangoel/Projects)

Simple projects to apply the language you learnt a while ago. One has an option to donate to the website for others to use. These open source projects will become wild card entry for building a successful career.

Step 5: Opportunities for Hire!

Participation and being in a community like the user group and meet up. Every topic in software has online user groups, both global and local.

1. Linux User Group and Bangalore Linux User Group.

2. There are User Groups for major languages such as Python, Java, Ruby and others. These groups usually do monthly meet ups to help the new entrants and present the latest topics in technology.

   For example, http://python.meetup.com.

3. Hackathon. For example, http://techcrunch-india.com/hackathon.html

4. Summer of Code (offered by Google) and other such events offered by other organizations

5. Conferences

6. Discussion Forums (stakexchange.com)

In order to reach diverse people, conferences conduct from groups from Java, Python, Javascript and others can be good places to get an interview call or to get hired. For example, http://hasgeek.com

Section 7

Case Study on Practice Testing and Programming

This is a controlled (supervised) exercise among students with a help of a supervisor. It is a common phenomenon for beginners to be too rigid to accept the feedback to make progress that would make training and practice as a continuous effort. We adopted Johari window (Joseph Luft and Harry Ingham) concept to help the participants identify their skills in recognizing and promoting individual points. The opinion of others about one's skills that defined you was reflected.

It works on two parameters: Knowing yourself and what others know about you. As a beginner, it's possible that participants think that they have adequate skills and others may not be aware of it. There are two outcomes to this area: others are made aware of one's talent or one gets to know the limitations. If the earlier is the case, one needs to showcase talents through presentation, demos and assumes roles to achieve the tasks. If latter is the case, receiving feedback from one's peer is a good way to start to build confidence and also early discovery of talents.

Objective: Intention of the activity was to teach software testing fundamentals in an unconventional (ways of learning programming) yet interactive manner.

The presentation was designed to include simple topics that would ultimately lead to understanding of the topics planned. Specific color combinations were used so that students get familiarized with the examples that relate to the specific topics.

The first exercise consisted of simple algebraic operations – addition and multiplication. The intention behind was to showcase the process to validate the data and it was observed that a sample batch was quick with it.

A simple problem was presented:

Problem 1:

Math - 90

Science - 85

Social - 95

Percentage - ?%

These were two interesting answers –

1. Is the dash a hyphen or a minus?
2. Some students guessed the answer as '90'.

It was concluded that one should not assume the total marks as 100. Perhaps a question should be asked, how many total marks are there for each subject?

The second exercise consisted of simple text, which consisted of one or several spelling mistakes. These were exercises that allowed students to quickly think and identify mistakes.

Problem 2:

I am attending the software testing intarective course...

The objective of the third exercise was to try escalating issues as it directly impacts the customer (user), and it consisted of scenarios like –

Problem 3:

If Facebook is down but you have to chat with your friend, what do you do?

These were two interesting answers –

1. Some suggested they would inform the chat about the issue via SMS or Phone.

2. Some suggested informing Facebook customer care.

These exercises have showcased that each one has their own perspective and testing is nothing but getting into shadows of various people and helping make the customer's life simpler and easier.

Activities

The above few exercises were done independently (Individual Contributor) and few activities were followed up to showcase the challenges in the work of a Program Manager (PM), Designer, Developer, Tester and others. Teams of two (PM, Designers and Developers) were made (randomly) and the following two tasks were given:

a. Construct a Five-Storey

b. Construct a boat

An analogy that seemed to be relevant to the students (that consisted mainly of women) was preparation of brinjal curry. Your mother-in-law would in all probability ask you to prepare the dish for 20 invited guests. Here, mother-in-law gives specs of Program

Manager. Your mother guides you for the kind of ingredients to add to get the expected taste of cooked curry. Here, mother's gives specs of Designer. You are a developer (to say), and your objective is preparing the curry for 20 guests from designer inputs.

Students juggled through various discussions, students did one round where PM gives spec, and then two designers drew sketches and developers implemented to construct boat or Five-storey building. Initially observations showed that the students were concerned about deadline (time allotment) but with more iteration the specs, designs and implementation were improved. These iterations helped students to understand what it meant to be a good tester and programmer.

Section 8

Short Profile of People in Computer Engineering Role with no Engineering Background

In this section, we bring you examples of four people who were not from Computer Engineering education background but have contributed to the software industry. Some examples here and else are a clear indication that Software Engineering is an interdisciplinary area to explore. What made these people successful? According to Richard St. John's, there are eight things -- Passion, Work, Serve, Focus, Persist, Ideas, Good, and Push — which are the secret to success. Software industry is all about incorporating these qualities as well.

1. Richard Stallman (GNU Projects)

2. Subroto Bagchi (Co-founder of Mindtree Ltd.)

3. Larry Wall (Creator of Perl Programming Language)

4. Sabeer Bhatia (Founder of Hotmail email)

Section 9

Impressions

There are two major impressions -- intrinsic and extrinsic -- that we leave the interviewer with. The intrinsic impressions are knowledge, attitude, aptitude and skills that are tested through the various interview rounds. Extrinsic impressions are as vital as intrinsic impressions; the degree of seriousness will vary from company to company. Although these extrinsic parameters are not evaluated as part of interview strategy by the earlier discussed companies, it is advisable to be over-prepared rather under-prepared. Let's look into an exhaustive listing of those impressions.

Punctuality: As this could be first visit to the company for an interview, it's good to familiarize yourself with the location and it always advisable to be on time for an interview.

Dress code: Conservative suits are still the accepted norms in some traditional offices and industries such as banking. Each company has appropriate guidelines to inform applicants about their desired dress code. If these look uncertain, it is advisable to overdress rather than underdress. It will convey a strong message that the applicant has put in special effort for the interview. Dress code can be broadly classified under traditional and casual business wear.

Traditional Business Wear
Men

Shirt: White or pale blue are preferred over bright colors or pattern ones.

Tie: Understated colors and patterns are preferred over bright colors and patterns.

Socks: Color that goes well along with the suit.

Shoes: Black or brown that goes with the suit. Clean and polished.

Suit: Cotton or wool, preferably in dark colors.

Briefcase: preferred over knapsack.

Women

Suit with skirt or pants: Cotton or wool one preferred in dark colors.

Blouse: Cotton or silk, ones with light or neutral color.

Shoes: Low-heel shoe that goes along with suit and handbag color. Clean and polished ones.

Stockings: Simple sheer skin-toned or black that goes with the skirt.

Jewelery: It is advised to keep it simple and understated.

Casual Business Wear
Men

Tops: Long-sleeved button-down shirts or plain shirts and a sweater.

Bottoms: Slacks or Khaki pants

(Although some companies are fine with Jeans or T-shirts or sandals, it's advisable to avoid these during interviews)

Women

Tops: Blouse, Dress shirt, Sweater, Jacket

Bottoms: Skirt, Pants

Hair: Clean, neat and away from your face is preferred.

Deodorant: Shower and use of deodorant is advisable before one appears for interviews.

Nails: Clean, clipped, and filed. While women may use clear or classic nail polish colors.

Mouth: Use of mouthwash or breath mints or brush could be handy as an interview could be a daylong affair.

Dinning Etiquette: As interviews are day affairs, it is likely an applicant may be invited over working breakfast and lunch or dinner at times. The ability to converse professionally with others as well table manners are crucial in such circumstances. Always follow the host's lead during dining. The above-mentioned companies may not have the interview member accompany the applicant, but it is always advisable to follow dining etiquette, as it's likely that the accompanying person may be a future colleague.

Drinks: It's fine to order a non-alcoholic drink to be on the safe side.

Food: Order or pick food that will allow the applicant to talk between bites. Avoid topics about politics, religion, personal, illness or non-relevant issues. Avoid chewing with mouth open or food in the mouth. Be the first to pass on any food to the host, this will leave a positive impression. Use one hand at a time for everything (such as bread, drinks) except for cutting food or taking a serving from a dish. Avoid slurping, especially while having soup. Always wait till the host starts eating.

Napkin: If it's a restaurant, place napkin on the lap. Avoids tucking it into the shirt or blouse. After meal, place the napkin on the left side of the plate. It is better to blot your lips rather than extensively wiping it.

Accidents: Accidents do happen during drinks or while eating. Apologize briefly and use extra napkins if needed. One need not dwell on the issue.

Tip at Table: Politeness (with others) is appreciated, use of 'please' and 'thank you' is appreciated.

Section 10

Resume Outline

"Interviewer looks in the interviewee shows"

In this section, an overview of resume preparation is provided. There is no single right methodology to prepare a resume; hence a process is explained to give a good perspective on resume preparation. Resume is similar to an advertising or marketing campaign to sell one's attributes to get hired for a specific role.

Prepare a Career Management Worksheet, that can consist of the following information –

1. Personal Information
2. Education
3. Vocational and Technical Training
4. Professional Development
5. References (Personal and Professional)
6. Essential Keywords

Once the above information is filled, a sample outline is provided in the next page for the readers to prepare a resume.

Rahul P. Varma
Mobile: email:

Profile

- B.E. Information Science major with extensive coursework and lab hours in programming (Java, .NET) and networking

- (Add more points if needed)

- (Add more points if needed)

Technical Skills
Languages (Add only if well versed)

Databases

Systems

Networking

Software

Others

Education
Dept. of Computer Science, National Institute of Technology Karnataka, Surathkal Anticipated July 2014

Major:

Coursework highlights:

Project (Add where, when and likely title)

(Open Source Projects would be given weightage)

-
-

Awards/Accomplishments (Add only relevant for the position)

(Papers and Publications)

-
-

References

1. Dave's Blog, 'CodeKata – How to Become a Better Developer', www.codekatak.com

2. Personal Computers: Does everyone need to learn programming?, Erik Sanberg-Diment, Jan 17, 1984, www.nytimes.com/1984/01/17/science/personal-computers-does-everyone-need-to-learn-programming.html

3. Why Software is Eating the World at WSJ.com

4. A complete Massive Open Online Courses http://www.mooc-list.com

5. www.stackoverflow.com

6. www.stackexchange.com

7. Hacker News : https://news.ycombinator.com/

Books (Highly recommended to read)

1. Hackers and Painters by Paul Graham

2. The Cathedral and The Bazaar by Eric S. Raymond

3. The Passionate Programmer by Chad Flower

4. The Pragmatic Programmer by Dave Thomas and Andy Hunt

5. CODE By Charles Petzold

6. The Architecture of Open Source Applications (Online edition http://aosabook.org/en/index.html)

Annexure 1: Ways to Learn

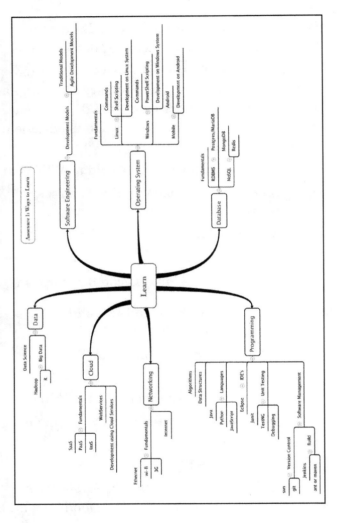

Annexure 2: How to Learn?

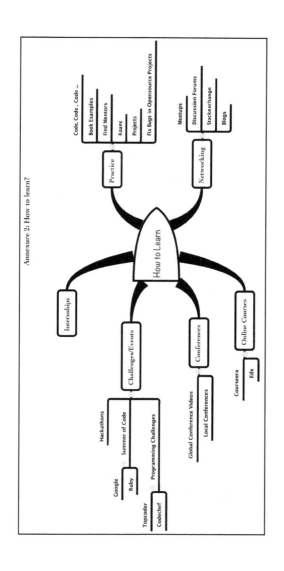

Annexure 2: How to learn?

Author's Profile

Santosh Avvannavar: Santosh started his career as a consultant and Soft Skills Trainer. After his college education from NITK, Surathkal, he worked as a researcher at University of Eindhoven, University of Twente, and Indian Institute of Science, Bangalore. He was also the Placement President while working at IISC, Bangalore. He has over twenty-five publications of mostly research documents in national and international journals. He has also authored sixteen conference papers and regularly writes articles for a national and worldwide daily paper. He also works as an advisor for different organizations.

He also dabbles in fiction writing and is the author of *Adhuri Prem Kahaniya; Dear Wife, Your Husband is not a Superhero* and *Second Heart*.

He likes to devote his personal time in writing for a website, namely the Amrita Foundation for HRD (www.amritafoundation.wordpress.com). He has conducted seminars and training sessions for more than 33,000 people in India and abroad over the last seven years.

Raghvendra R: Raghavendra has 17+ years of experience in various roles like developer, system admin, and test engineer in companies like i2, HP, Yahoo! Love OpenSource and educating others on Software Programming and Testing.

Thank you for reading our book. If you enjoyed it, would you please take a moment to leave us a review at your favorite retailer?

Thanks,
Santosh Avvannavar
Ragvendra R

DISCLAIMER: We are not trained human resource or certified professionals. We're just average folks who understand what it is takes to make a career in the twenty-first century. The information presented here is like a mentor to guide aspiring IT applicants. The software industry is relatively new and undergoing constant changes; we highly recommend our readers check the career sections of the companies to get the latest updates.

www.ingramcontent.com/pod-product-compliance
Lightning Source LLC
Chambersburg PA
CBHW071010050326
40689CB00014B/3560